"Philippa Kingsley's book offers a truly heartfelt and deeply personal account of her encounters with grief. You will be touched by her courage and honesty. True compassion lies at the heart of grief."

—Dale Borglum, The Living/Dying Project, co-author of *Journey of Awakening*

"This book will not only connect you with your own experience of grief but shines a light for others who are struggling to come to terms with the loss of a person or pet."

—Colin Tipping, author of *Radical Forgiveness* and *Radical Self-Forgiveness*

RISING ABOVE GRIEF
for People and Pets

A True Story of
LOVE, SHARING, AND CARING

By

Philippa Kingsley

BALBOA.
PRESS
A DIVISION OF HAY HOUSE

ISBN: 978-1-4525-5500-3 (sc)
ISBN: 978-1-4525-5501-0 (e)
Library of Congress Control Number: 2012911729

Balboa Press books may be ordered through booksellers or by contacting:

Balboa Press
A Division of Hay House
1663 Liberty Drive
Bloomington, IN 47403
www.balboapress.com
1-(877) 407-4847

Printed in the United States of America

Balboa Press rev. date: 07/31/2012

This book is dedicated to my darling father and beloved dogs.

TABLE OF CONTENTS

ACKNOWLEDGEMENTS

LOVE AND LIGHT TO ALL WHO HAVE HELPED ME ON MY PATH TO AWAKEN TO ALL THAT IS

There is no "running order" of importance to those mentioned here. Each one is special and important at different times, different stages, and in different ways. Some of the people are aware of the part they have played in my life to date, and some are not. It doesn't matter. I love you all and always will from the bottom of my heart. Forget the egoic mind; there is just Divine Love. Remember this:

People come into your life for a reason, a season, or a lifetime.

Firstly, I thank the Divine, Merlin, and the Angelic realm for showing me everything that I needed to learn for my growth on this earth at this time, and also for channeling this book through me. I thank my darling father and beloved dogs, who are in spirit, for all the love and support that they always give me from the other dimensions of time and space.

Thank you to all the VortexHealing® Divine Energy Healing teachers: Ric Weinman, holder of the lineage; Anthony Gorman; Lorraine Goldbloom, Alexandra Marquardt; and Gailynn Carroll. www.vortexhealing.org

I am grateful for the angelic inspiration of Doreen Virtue, and for esteemed animal communicator and legendary teacher, Penelope Smith, who lives true to herself. Thank you, David Hand, physic and medium: we were meant to connect.

Diana Jones, my dearest spiritual friend in London, was the catalyst for guiding me to the power of the Angelic realm, and later guided me to discover VortexHealing® Divine Energy Healing. There is no co-incidence in anything in life.

Thank you to my wonderful and brilliant editor of this book, Karen Adler. The moment Karen and I spoke, I knew she was the right person for editing the book. She understood the deep spiritual essence of what was needed, as she had edited and published a metaphysical magazine.

We understood each other, and both have great humor, which is an asset in any relationship. She understood that it had to be my voice, although I decided that British grammar or phraseology had to be translated to American! She sometimes pushed me out of my comfort zone to think outside of what I thought was right, and made me see a different viewpoint or way of looking at a sentence or paragraph. You have to be able to let go and be vulnerable, otherwise you cannot move forward.

Surrender and release: these were the first things that I had to do, when I sent her the draft chapters of the book. I remember her telling me that I would write some more chapters; I didn't agree, but she was right. Six weeks later I was channeled four extra chapters! A bond and a lasting friendship has ensued from this writing and editing process.

Love and thank you to my friends and family in London…

My friends, Jean and Anthony Halperin, you are a safe haven in heaven! And these dear friends, spanning the eras: Molly Sher, Jacquie Rapaport, Suzie Garland, Penny Bannerman, Derry Treanor, Terry Tan, and George Ashmore, as well as Wanee Tipchindachaikul, my Thai friend in Bangkok, and from many lifetimes, who I met in London.

Much love to my dear brother Richard, and my wonderful caring, loving sister-in-law Marion—the best sister-in-law that one can ever have.

Thank you to my cousins, Pam Millard, Keith Bragman, and Jo Manuel, for all their loving support; I also treasure my special relationship and bond with Saul Bragman, and a growing friendship with Claudia Bragman.

In the USA...

Barbara Rubin and family, including their dogs, Chakra, Roxy, Rasta, and Lulu, you all hold a special place in my heart. Barbara has been my surrogate family and sister here in Atlanta since 1996.

And much love and appreciation to Diane Saulson, a loyal and caring friend; Tip Weniger, my dear Thai friend and mentor; and Bernard Cohen, loyal and loving always. And to Manuela de Groot, Voguie & Cosmo's second mummy—thank you to a nurturing and caring friend. To our neighbor, Linda Slovic—your dog, Dukie, together with my dogs Voguie and Cosmo, cemented the bonds of our close friendship and sisterly love.

Samara Cummins: we met in London, and will always be connected wherever we live. Love and thanks to my aunt, Ena McClure, also to my cousin David King, for a friendship built from the family bond, and to my dear spiritual friend Teresa Wells, for a long term connection and friendship: to be able to share and connect with no judgment is beautiful to behold; to Candace Apple, from Phoenix and Dragon bookstore, who believes in me; and Jamie Butler, connection.

I am grateful to Stephen Walker, the graphic designer who thinks "outside the box" with his creativity; to Erin Brauer, the photographer who contributed her skill and talent to produce the photographs of me in my garden—they are fabulous; to Dawn Klempf, for positive enrichment; and to Cathy Apodaca from Sante Fe.

I have left it to last to acknowledge three special people:

My mother, my mother-in-law and Martin.

My dearest delicate mother Betty, a gentle butterfly needing to find her wings to fly to new heights. Sadly, she is now in a world of her own with Alzheimer's disease, leaving me with the realization that love is truly all there is.

My mother-in-law, Leona Perel: We share a very special bond. She always believed in me well before I ever believed in myself.

My darling husband Martin Perel. A gentle artistic soul, a true artisan, a loving and lovable sweet man with a kind caring disposition, always willing to help and explore. I always knew that we were connected from previous lifetimes, which is why we are together in this life. The universe sent him from Cape Town to me in London, via The Netherlands, disregarding geographic distance. When Divine timing strikes the gong we move to the dance of its beat. As we go through life's challenges together we meld and grow, putting down roots, with the powerful statement that in life Divine love transcends all.

RISING ABOVE GRIEF

Dedicated to my darling father and beloved dogs
For the lessons learned

INTRODUCTION

I have been guided in spirit to share my innermost thoughts and channeled writings of the experience of loss, letting go, and transitions from the physical body of my darling father and beloved pets.

I am guided to help others who are suffering, or have suffered, while walking down the road of grief, with the realization that there is a beginning, a middle, and an end to this process, and with the awareness that you too will rise above grief and learn to live and laugh again.

Where is my mother's voice? I am her voice. Grief manifests in different forms, as my mother is trapped in her physical body, in a timeless state of mindless limbo. Alzheimer's disease is her challenge and ours.

Since 1986, I have been on a quest for the spiritual grail which is within all of us, if we choose. VortexHealing® Divine Energy Healing, together with Angelic guidance, was the catalyst for my realization and awakening to All That Is, enabling me to love, care, and share with people and pets.

VortexHealing® Divine Energy Healing is about change and the transformation of consciousness at the root causal level, healing issues originating from the mental, physical, emotional, spiritual and karmic levels, enabling people to let go of old patterns and ways of thinking that bind and blind them to their true purpose in this life. It works at the cellular level, releasing issues of fear and lack of self-worth, which are the bases of most people's *dramas*. VortexHealing® Divine Energy Healing also helps people to forgive themselves or a situation, lightening the load that they have been carrying in their system. VortexHealing®️ Divine Energy Healing is more than just a healing process; it opens and deepens the spiritual heart, enabling a ripening process to occur—allowing awakening.

Channeled writing, for me, is akin to radio waves of energy on different frequencies that come through me, guiding me to write. It's like when the channel is changed on a television or radio. I am channeled with thought patterns from higher realms of consciousness–my spiritual guides, archangels, father, and pets, all guiding me to write down what comes through my mind. This happens to me at any time and anywhere. My channeled writings commenced in 2005.

ABOUT PHILIPPA

Philippa Kingsley began a spiritual quest in 1986. Her search culminated in her discovery of an ancient healing art called VortexHealing® Divine Energy Healing, as well as Angelic guidance, as the catalysts for her realization and awakening to All That Is. Originally from London, Philippa lived in The Netherlands for four years, where she became a professional Thai chef and instructor, and founded a unique Thai catering company and Thai cooking school, Philippa's Orient.

Philippa personally experienced the transformative power of VortexHealing® Divine Energy Healing with a deep-seated family issue that she thought would never change. It was through this experience that she became committed to sharing this healing process with others.

In 1996, she and her husband, Martin, moved to Atlanta, Georgia, along with their two English Cocker Spaniels, Voguie and Cosmo. A self-confessed "dogaholic," Philippa began cooking organic food for her dogs and any other dogs that happened to be around the house at feeding time. She loves cats, too, as well as all other companion animals.

Voguie left this world in September 2004, after a three month bout of kidney failure, during which Philippa went through the depths of despair. The emotional journey that everyone in the family went through, including Cosmo, was debilitating. Even more emotional challenges came up in 2009, the year that Philippa lost her darling father in May, and in October, Cosmo transitioned from her physical body after a battle with cancer.

Knowing and understanding the grief process, combined with the journey of holistic and spiritual healing, has given Philippa the basis and understanding to help people and pets through Love, Sharing, and Caring. She has developed a diverse client base of adults, children, and animals, and regularly speaks publicly about VortexHealing® Divine Energy Healing. Philippa provides private VortexHealing® Divine Energy Healing sessions, teaches meditation classes, and specializes in animal communication, providing pet grief counseling, work with rescue pets, and guidance around health issues.

Philippa Kingsley is a certified VortexHealing® Divine Energy Healing practitioner, animal communicator, certified past life healer, certified Reiki practitioner, and a certified member of The National Association of Public Speakers and Trainers. To learn more about Philippa's classes and individual consultations, please visit www.healingpeopleandpets.com.

1. VEIL OF ILLUSION

Channeled in my kitchen December 29, 2008

*As the Veil of Illusion is swept away like a tidal wave
now we can take time to reflect,
look at what is reality and what is not.
We can live in the Now
Enjoy all that is meant for our personal growth,
accepting and awakening to the predicament of the earth.*

It's about change and transformation of the consciousness of each of us at a cellular level.

It takes time to admit that the way we have been living has been detrimental to our health and our soul's journey. It takes great strength of character and courage to stand up and say, *enough.* What seemingly worked for years is no longer valid or true.

My analogy is of the snake: The snake sheds its skin, slithers along the ground. You take yourself with you wherever you live in the world, whatever country, town, city, or state, but you are still the essence of you. It's just the old skin that withers away so that you can fully embrace the might and majesty of your inner soul.

Two quotations resonate with me on the subject of illusion:

The only thing permanent in life, is impermanence.

Gautama Buddha

Tradition is an illusion for permanence.

Woody Allen

1

2. LOVE IS

Channeled May 21, 2006
For my friend Aleta on the occasion of her engagement

LOVE IS

Knowing that you are there for me.

Knowing that I am there for you.

Come rain or shine… Come what may

we pledge our souls to each other for this time on earth.

LOVE IS

Knowing that we were connected before in another time and place.

Knowing that our paths are intertwined and lessons learned.

Knowing that now we grow together, the lessons for the future shared

the power of one becomes stronger when there are two.

LOVE IS

Knowing that I am loved.

Knowing that you are loved.

From the depths of the soul.

Just the knowing.

The instinct that our spiritual journey at this time in our lives

brought us just to this place to take us onto the next dimension.

LOVE IS

Knowing that in the mental, physical, emotional, and spiritual sphere

All is One and One is All.

3. ESSENCE OF SPIRITUALITY

Channeled in my office May and June 2011

Do you realize that the true essence of spirituality comes from within ourselves, not from the outer trappings of life? Any change comes from within and manifests out into the world. We can all experience the essence of pure Divine love running through our whole being. And we can experience the uplifting of the soul as it navigates the challenging and treacherous path of life and suffering, with the realization that there is a way out of this. It's up to us. As human beings we are all given free will. Choices: you can take the left path or the right, with the basic premise that it's you deciding to commit to yourself.

Your commitment to yourself is defined by these questions: *Do I deserve? Am I worthy enough? Am I good enough? Do I choose to make the time to do something about it?*

Busy being busy seems to be the daily mantra for many people who choose to opt out of the commitment to themselves. We learn that having no time for ourselves, no time for anyone, or anything else, puts our minds and our bodies in extreme stress mode, which often manifests into physical illness or the decision to pop a pill as a quick fix.

At this time on the earth's plane, we are being challenged on so many levels. It's happening all around us at such a fast pace. Look around you, to Japan, the Middle East, climate change, and in our midst, the unresolved global financial crisis, affecting us all. Newspapers, radio, TV, the Internet all sell us fear, and we feed into that fear. This is why at this time it's important to stay grounded, put -down roots.

Think of a tree. We notice the parts that are above ground. We see the trunk, we see the branches. They sway gracefully in the wind, with luscious leaves so beautiful to behold in their spring and fall colors, or weakened branches breaking and falling. What we tend to forget is the most important thing of all, the roots. We don't see them above ground, but they are the foundation for the tree's strength and growth. So it is with the human being. The roots have to be nourished and watered or they dry up, wither and die. Wake up as to why you need to put down roots and *water* yourself. My mantra for you: *nourishment, not punishment!*

So many people are disconnected from themselves and what is real. Some people have a total disorientation of their body to themselves and what is going on internally. There has to be balance and harmonious alignment between the mental, physical, emotional, spiritual, and karmic bodies for everything to work as one.

For a while, I hadn't realized that my physical body was also depleted from all the spiritual energy I was giving out to other people. I took steps to help my physical body heal with VortexHealing energy and meditations to strengthen and align the force within to become One.

CALLING ALL WOMEN–THE DIVINE FEMININE

For women, it's important to realize that we tend to negate and undermine our strengths. It's time to take back our original sense of our inner feminine truth. Learn to love ourselves, realize our strength and power with inner awareness, and trust that we have everything that we need at a core level. If we impact our minds with negative thoughts then that is what we will attract. We can control the mind and ego. Our ego doesn't want us to change; it's had the same pattern for many lifetimes. Only we can release the fear and pain of this life by changing our core orientation, the causal level of issues that are stored in our cellular system.

As the Buddha taught, we can listen to this learned person, listen to that learned person, but to walk the middle way, walk the middle path. Make our own choices.

Society pre-judges people and our actions. In fact, we need to look back into history, as all the lessons are there for us to learn in this modern world. We tend to think that we know it all, however it's only the style of clothes and culture that changes. Take away the veneer and image of respectability, and you are left with the awareness that human beings and human nature are the same now as in previous generations, down through the centuries. Remember, we come into this world with nothing and we leave with nothing. Money, power, and greed do not define our success. It's what we choose do in the middle timeline of our lives that defines our legacy.

Look into your heart, look into your soul, and choose wisely. The choice is yours.

MY FATHER

4. AN INSPIRATIONAL STORY

Channeled through me in 2007

My father, who was a physician and surgeon in London, had two brain surgeries in 2005. He survived that ordeal.

In 2006, he was diagnosed with colon cancer and had part of his colon removed. In the United Kingdom he was considered too old to have chemotherapy. In October 2006, he had a bowel obstruction and was rushed to hospital as an emergency. He then stopped eating.

I had been backward and forward between Atlanta and London, on an intense emotional roller coaster. I rushed to London, fearing the worst.

Nobody, not the specialist, the nursing staff, my brother, and not even my father himself, thought he would survive. My mother has Alzheimer's disease and just withdrew emotionally, as it was too painful for her to see my usually strong father in this condition.

My father did not want to eat or drink. No offer of food, even his favorites, could entice him, and he had always been a foodie, like me! I had invested in a juicer, which was housed at my parents' home, but he still refused everything. It was so difficult to watch him literally wasting away to skin and bones. I moved into the hospital and slept in his room, and concentrated all my time with him for two weeks. During this time I did VortexHealing on my father.

There has always been a deep karmic emotional bond between us, but we had become disengaged over the years, and with me living abroad, it did not make it any easier, due to the distance factor. On this earth, we think we have a time-frame, but the universe doesn't. Time doesn't mean anything on the higher realms. The impact of the reality of the situation for us both enabled me to become mother and daughter, rolled into one. We talked, we cried, we laughed, and we finally became one with each other on a truthful acceptance of things that were, things that are, and things that will be. We forgave each other and certain situations, realizing the essence of life is so pure and that you have to let go to move on.

We both realized how lucky we were to have been given the gift of cleansing our hearts and our souls so that we could move onto the next dimension.

I had to leave London to return to my life in Atlanta. Both our hearts were breaking when it came time to say goodbye. We both thought we would never see each other again.

The hospital sent my father home. Eventually he started to eat again, but his whole system was extremely sluggish, and he was so thin and weak; just a shadow of his former self, who had always been energetic, charismatic, and a dedicated doctor, beloved by all his patients.

A crisis arose when he hadn't been to the bathroom for one week. He was given all the medical assistance to help his system move. Just before they were going to administer the last drastic ammunition in the arsenal, I phoned from Atlanta, spoke to my sister-in-law and said, *"Use the juicer."* I had been nagging for weeks about juicing, but it had been falling on deaf ears. In the end, everyone was so desperate they used the juicer with my recipe; lo and behold, it worked immediately!

As for my darling father, he is juicing every day, has put on weight, and is eating normally. His voice sounds strong and he is motivated to fully ingest life. We both know that he was given another chance. How old is he? Eighty-seven years young!

There is no coincidence in life; everything happens for a reason, although we don't always know at the time. When you have a life-threatening illness, you change your views and your priorities in life. My father was able to make his peace with himself, and with his life. We were able to make peace with one another. It takes time to realize that life is a gift and that there are other healing options available. Never give up, keep faith, trust and belief in yourself. Things come to you in life when they are meant to be. Accept with open arms and learn to live each day in the present moment.

5. GRIEF AND SURRENDER TO ALL THAT IS:

DEATH WITH DIGNITY

I am guided in spirit to share my channeled writings with you about my darling father, Dr. Sidney Kingsley, and his transition from his physical body. These channelings took place in May and June 2009.

My Sidney, my Father, my Darling, left his physical body on Monday, May 4, 2009 at 1:00 pm (lunchtime).

At my parents' home, lunch was always at 1:00 pm on the dot. This was also the time that my father chose to leave his physical body. I wasn't in the room for this, but was driving like James Bond in a frantic rush to get back to the hospice. It was a Bank Holiday in London and I had rushed to find lunch for myself. A nurse called me and told me to return to the hospice urgently.

I wanted to see the physical moment when the soul leaves the body, but had been warned by the nurses that you can just turn your back for a moment or leave the room, and the soul can leave the body. It can also be very difficult for the person dying to have distractions from family around them at the moment of transition. It was not meant to be for me to see this actual moment. I arrived back at the hospice at 1:07 pm.

I had been mounting a vigil, but the night before my father died, I just couldn't sleep in his room, even though his nurse had set up a folding bed next to his bed. I chose to curl up in a fetal ball, snuggled under a big white hospital duvet in an alcove just outside his room. One nurse who got on with me very well gave me some hospice pajamas, and I joked with her, "Make sure you don't get me muddled up with a patient and give me morphine!"

The Rabbi had been and gone; he had told me that my father was not ready to leave his body that night. The Rabbi said the Shemah prayer over my father and somehow this was all part of the process of leaving the physical body. My father was not a practicing Jew, but sometimes we all need rites of passage to help us on our way.

I had rushed to London from Atlanta, knowing that this was the final curtain in the play that was unfolding before my eyes. My father had fallen at home, was taken to hospital and was told that the colon cancer had spread to his bones and vital organs. He was 89 years old, and as a doctor, he knew the medical prognosis. He stayed in hospital for a few days until my brother and I found a hospice for him.

My father and I had a bond that will never be broken; it transcends time and space. Karmic bonds and a shared lineage from eons ago.

"Je t'aime toujours." The beautiful French words, *I will love you always.*

"Moi aussi," I replied. *Me too.*

These were the words that he spoke to me. He held my hand and took it to his lips, a true gesture of deep love, and spoke those beautiful eternal words in French, in the middle of a busy, bustling hospital ward. There we were, the two of us, it was as if we were in a bubble of time, it was as if time had stood still. Where did the French come from? It came from the depths of his soul from a previous lifetime. French is the language of lovers. I couldn't control the flow of tears. Forever, the deep love shared.

At the hospice, when my father had transitioned from his physical body, I had arranged that I wanted to sit with his body. Hours later, he was moved to a special room, which was kept ice cold. This change became very traumatic for me and one of my cousins had unexpectedly arrived to support me with the transition to the room. She had also experienced great loss and understood the implications of grief. The special Orthodox Burial Society was not going to arrive until the next day, as it was a Bank Holiday. Again, I had previously arranged that I wanted to sit with my father all day and night. Again, there is no co-incidence.

I now sat all night in the ice cold room, muffled up in blankets. When I sat with the shell of my father, his soul had physically left his body and had transitioned to a higher plane. The tears welled up from deep inside me. I cried, and I spoke to him, even though he was not in his physical body. There is a general belief that the soul stays around for two to three days after death.

I said the same words to him that he had spoken to me.

"Je t'aime toujours, je t'aime toujours, je t'aime toujours."

"Moi aussi, moi aussi, moi aussi."

I understood then and I understand now that the cycle of love can never break.

Pure love transcends all. To have had the chance to experience the transition of the soul, to be with my beloved father, happened as it was meant to happen.

The pain that death unleashes is immense. Even when you think you are prepared for the eventual transition, when the reality hits you are not actually prepared. The conscious mind wants the loved one to find a release from all the physical suffering of the body, and you think you have said goodbye and done all you can. Now the realization occurs that it is just an empty shell there with you in the room. The cold hands is how it starts, the withdrawal from the world. I read about it and thought I understood it, but I realized I didn't. You put your hand on the heart and there is nothing there. The soul has gone; just a shell is left.

The final testament of love was to be at the burial ground. When a Jewish person dies, the Burial Society carry out a ritualistic bathing of the body, and prayers are recited. Even though my father wasn't religious, it had been arranged for him to be buried in an Orthodox cemetery. The Orthodox Jewish ruling is based on a patriarchal form of tradition. In the past, women were not allowed to attend funerals. Thankfully, in the modern world this has changed, and it is up to women to decide in what form to participate.

During the time that my father was in the hospice I had arranged with the Burial Society that I would be able to see my father for one last time before the coffin was nailed down prior to the funeral ceremony. My brother did not want to participate in this, as it was too emotionally upsetting for him. As I say, each person manifests grief in their own personal way.

The morning of the burial came. Early May in London, the weather could still be unreliable, but it was a crisp bright day. I drove myself early to the burial grounds in order to see my darling father's face for one last time. One of my cousins, also a doctor, was there to greet me. I was happy for his physical presence and emotional support.

I was transfixed with my gaze on my beloved father in his coffin, wrapped in a white shroud and his prayer shawl, called a *tallis*. I needed this special time with him. There was nothing else to say; it was just to take in every moment of this momentous mountain of love that arose in me.

The men and a rabbi from the Burial Society came into the room. It was now time to close the coffin and nail down the lid. Prayers were said, and I asked that the final ritual of love for my father would be for me to put some earth from Jerusalem into the coffin with him. In Israel people are not put into coffins, they are put directly into the earth in a shroud; men are wrapped in their prayer shawls. Outside of Israel a Jewish burial coffin is made of wood. The person is buried facing towards the east. Earth from Jerusalem, home of the Temple Mount, one of the holiest sites in the world, is put in the coffin, symbolizing that there is no barrier between earth and body. The body goes back to the earth and the soul returns to Source.

After adding the earth and being allowed to help with the nailing down of the coffin lid, I suddenly became calm and still, and knew that this whole process with the coffin was a karmic rite of passage that

I had just finished with my father. I did not feel like crying, I did not feel sadness, just a feeling of knowing that it was the final curtain of a karmic cycle and bond that my father and I had always shared. My final gift to my father had been given in the physical form, but on a higher level and dimension, a karmic debt had been paid.

The funeral took place shortly afterwards. I know that family and friends seem surprised that I was so calm and that I was able to read out the words that I had written for my beloved father. They did not know or understand the enormity of the whole process that had just unfolded and what had transpired prior to the closing of the coffin.

The mind knows and can see but the emotional body cannot quite take it all in. This is the beginning of grief and mourning the loss.

The pain of emptiness. I am empty, Oh so empty.

At times it totally consumes and engulfs. I know that I have to move through all the stages of grief. This mental, physical, emotional, and spiritual experience, it paralyzes you.

Every time I sleep, I dream. Dream all aspects of loss and letting go. I cannot remember all the content of the dreams, just the vivid emotions around loss and letting go. The only thing that gives me comfort is the hospice Teddy Bear that my cousin bought for me. Just cuddling the stuffed toy transports me back to the realms of my childhood. I cuddle the bear when I go to sleep; it's what I need at this time. Age is irrelevant, a grown woman clutching a bear. We take comfort from whence it is offered.

His voice is still on my answer phone in Atlanta, a message from February 2008. On some level I knew, even then, and made a conscious decision to keep the message. I have his watch, signet ring, dressing gown from Harrods that he loved to wear, and yellow waistcoat, all with me in Atlanta.

But he is not here, yet I know he is with me. At the moment, like mine, his soul is resting after the immense transition and release from his physical form. I am resting too. When the time is right he will come to me in a dream. He is forever in my heart, he is part of me. For now I feel the pain, I am so lethargic, nothing interests me. What was important before no longer is. I am paralyzed, and find it so difficult to function. I am living day to day in the moment and am nurturing myself.

I have learned to surrender to all that is. Nothing else matters at all. Love is all there is and endures forever.

I never had any prior experience of a hospice. On behalf of my darling father, Dr. Sidney Kingsley, all I can say is that the dignity of a hospice makes the process of dying dignified. Thank you all the Sisters and Nurses at Peace Hospice, Peace Drive, Watford, England, for the loving, caring and sharing that you do.

6. RISING ABOVE GRIEF

LOVE, CARING, AND SHARING

Channeled April 10, 2011

The soul is but an actor upon the stage of life. The stage set is life, and the soul makes a pact with the Divine Director. Who is this Director? The Divine. Oneness with All That Is.

LOVE, CARING, and SHARING: We as humans have forgotten the essence of these words and are so used to running round in a shallow quest for materialism that we have created for ourselves.

The year of 2009 was particularly emotionally challenging for me. I lost my darling father in May and my beloved dog, Cosmo in October. I am guided in spirit to share my innermost thoughts to help others who are suffering through the process of grief.

It's now two years since my darling father Sidney transitioned from his physical body. Only now can I put pen to paper to release the final grief and sadness that had been held tightly in place, and is now like a snake unfurling itself from a tightly coiled sleep.

All the time, I was channeled with thoughts and a deep knowing of everything unfolding at the pace that it was meant to be, and I gave myself full permission to grieve. The total process of loss and grief brings the realization that once our loved ones have left their bodies, we who are left behind on this physical realm are the ones who find it so hard to let go, even though we know that our loved ones are no longer suffering.

Once we have experienced the death of a loved one for the first time, there is a gradual understanding that nothing will ever be the same again. We have gained entry to an exclusive club, with the guarantee of a lifetime membership.

We humans are the ones who continue to suffer, as that is part of the human legacy. It takes great strength and courage to let go and realize that grief is a process. We who live in the West are so conditioned to a sterile death, usually in a sterile hospital bed hooked up to machines, monitors, and hospital restrictions.

I have total respect and admiration for hospice and the people who work there. When entering hospice, the patient has a prognosis of being terminally ill. The decision has been made to end medical intervention, except to relieve pain and keep the patient as comfortable as possible. In hospice, you are cocooned and lovingly cared for; families can bond and say their farewells in a safe, loving space. I liken the hospice experience to being softly blown in by a gentle gust of wind; you gently float along until a stronger gust of wind propels and pushes you out *the other side.* It's such a delicate process, you are not consciously aware of it at the time; it's the afterthought that comes to mind at a later date.

Up until the last one hundred years or so, people were born at home and died at home. Most people experienced the beginning and the end of the cycle of life and death, surrounded by loved ones that welcomed them into the world, followed by the shared experience at the end of the passage of life, surrounded by beloved family and friends. Later, the whole town or village would take part in the funeral rites.

During the era of Queen Victoria of England, often called the Victorian era, people celebrated and accepted death. Queen Victoria lost her beloved Prince Albert, and instead of grieving privately, showed the world their love and devotion to each other with a State funeral. Others were inspired to follow her funery example, with black carriages, black horses with matching black plumes, and interments in mausoleums, which became part of the culture of death at that time.

In ancient Egypt, the Afterlife culture took precedence over life in the here and now. The Pharaohs built pyramids. Burial tombs and chambers with interior colors of turquoise and terra cotta with mummification were *de rigueur* for burial. The organs were mummified separately and kept in separate pots from the mummy. There would be food offerings for the journey to the Other Side, along with gold, jewelry, precious stones, and anything valuable that was deemed necessary for the journey. Cats were highly revered, and they, too, were buried with their beloved master or mistress after they died.

In the Far East death is not feared; it is accepted as part of life's natural cycle, like the ebb and flow of water gently undulating on the shore of the ocean. Families united in the letting go process tend to lean on each other and talk about their feelings. Even when there is an understanding of the process of leaving the physical body, there is still the grief process to transcend. In some areas of the Far East, the physical body is not cremated immediately. For example, in Thailand, family, friends, and monks celebrate their loved ones with music, prayers, and food offerings for anywhere from seven to one hundred nights prior to cremation, dependent on the status in society.

So you see, it doesn't matter which belief system you resonate with, it's just the fact that you feel as you feel. Religion is there for the rite of passage, whether it's birth, marriage, or death. The grieving process offers no finite rite of passage–just the realization that however you want or need to grieve, that is the process that you have to go through. The need to grieve manifests differently in each person; there is no set pattern or timeline.

When one hears the diagnosis of a loved one who has a life-threatening illness, the shock and disbelief translates into a total nightmare of initial fear. When one is given a timeline to digest the news there are different ways of dealing with it.

This knowledge initiates a form of pre-grieving. It's something that the mind knows it will have to deal with at a future date, but a form of blanking off occurs, too. There is the awareness in the subconscious mind and in all the cells—an awareness of an imminent feeling of loss, but not of the total reality of the situation. This is something that I became aware of with my father's diagnosis of colon cancer.

The same effect transpired with Cosmo's diagnosis, too. Somehow your loved one will always be there, except that they won't always be there in physical form. Although we know that we will all have to leave our physical body, it always seems to be at some time in the future. Eventually we have to face it; the future becomes the now.

There is also the other side of the spectrum, with people who suddenly leave their physical body through a heart attack, accident or war. The pre-grieving doesn't occur, because it was totally unexpected. As humans, we don't know how long we have in this physical form, in this physical world, which has the densest energy of all the realms. This is why we need to nurture each other, love each other, care for each other.

Tell whoever you have in your life that you love them. Sometimes the people we have in our lives are unemotional, cold, or distant. However, sometimes it's not what you say, it's how you say it. One day what you say may just get through to them. It doesn't help if, after the event, you have guilt that you should have said something nice. There is not always a tomorrow, but there is always NOW. Live in the moment, as you will never have that moment again. Don't live in the past; you can't change the past, you learn from it. Some people totally live in the future; it's fine to make plans, but as we have learned, and are learning, things can be pulled out from under us. Prime examples are the 2011 earthquake, then tsunami, that hit Japan, as well as the political uprisings in the Middle East. The earth is making us aware at this time, through global warming and the ramifications arising from it, of cause and effect, the law of karma.

Therefore, for me, I am lucky that my father and I had time to say everything that we wanted and needed to say to each other.

There is no more time, there is just *NOW*. It's called *LOVE, CARING, AND SHARING.*

MY PETS

7. LOSING YOUR BELOVED PET

I am guided in Spirit by my beloved pets Voguie and Cosmo to help you deal with the emotional earthquake called grief that follows the loss of a beloved pet.

These channelings of Divine Love will help you at this challenging time and show you that you are not alone in your grief. So many people feel the same intense pain of loss and physical separation when our pets transition from their physical bodies. The manifestation of the grief process is different for everyone, but the root cause is the same. It's not something that you learn in textbooks, but the actual experience catapults you to a totally different dimension of your inner being that perhaps you never knew existed.

Grief and Grieving—a noun and a verb. A verb is a *doing* word, and so it is with grieving. Grief and Grieving is a process that we have to go through that enables us to come out the other end, stronger and more able to deal with ourselves and life. It's irrelevant whether the pet is a four legged, two legged, furry, or feathered being, loss is loss and grief is grief. There are people who choose not to deal with the grieving process, and consciously opt out of thinking and feeling. However, at some future intersection of their lives it will catch up with them with even more intensity.

When you know that your pet has a life-threatening illness and you know the long-term diagnosis, a form of grieving commences. Perhaps you are backwards and forwards to the vet, trying different approaches, which may be traditional, holistic, or a mixture. The realization is there, but you do not quite want to believe it, and a *blanking off* process begins. It's like not wanting to lift the veil on the truth, even though you know you will have to deal with it at a future juncture.

It's so important to surround yourself with people who truly understand you and what you are going through. Your partner, spouse, or close friends may not truly understand the intense feelings of loss that you are experiencing. Some people may say, *It's only a dog*, *It's only a cat*, *Get over it*, or *Get a new one*. These words are spoken without clear thinking. Your pet is not something that you can just throw out in the trash, then go down the street and buy a new one. It's important to take time to grieve the loss of your beloved pet. Put some distance between yourself and people who truly don't understand your feelings at this time. You are emotionally fragile, therefore, don't let yourself be manipulated or pushed into anything that doesn't resonate with you at a core level.

***

HELPFUL HEALING TOOLS

There is no set pattern of what to do. Anything you feel drawn to do is right for you at this time.

Have a Burial Ritual

If you have a burial at home, or scattering of ashes if your pet was cremated, involve all your family and friends. It's a form of honoring your beloved pet and what they meant to you. If you have written a letter or poem, choose to share it at this time. Any kind of ritual helps us acknowledge the love that was shared by all.

Help Children Understand and Say Goodbye

If you have children, and have to say goodbye to your beloved pet at the vet's office or have the vet come to your home, involve your children, as they need to understand the process of grief, which is part of life. By gently explaining euthanasia to your children, you take away their fear. It is important to acknowledge their feelings.

Express Yourself in Writing

Write a letter or a poem to your beloved pet and keep it. Writing is cathartic and will help you release your emotional pain, especially as you can just let the thoughts flow through the pen.

Make a Memorial

Find an area in your home that feels comfortable for you. Set up a small table or chest and put out favorite pictures, a candle that stays lit for one week (metaphysical book stores are a good source--white is for purity and a perfect choice), collar, leash, or anything personal, a flower or plant. You will know what to do when you start this process. If you have children, involve them in this process. You are a family and it will help strengthen bonds and communication about your beloved pet.

Pay Attention to Your Other Pets

Realize too that animals who have lived with the pet that has transitioned also grieve. It's important to pay attention to their wants and needs. They also have to deal with our human grief along with the loss of their friend. It's always important for all members of a family to say goodbye, and this relates to all the animals in your family, too.

Honor and Release Your Feelings

If you feel like screaming, do so. Give yourself permission to emit a gut-wrenching cry from the depths of your soul, which will help release the pent-up emotions and pain. I'm not suggesting that you do this in front of your family or friends. There's always the garden, the car, the park, the ocean, river, or many other places that I haven't mentioned.

Take Good Care of Yourself

It's important to nurture yourself at this time. Take a long luxurious soak in the bath, surrounded by candles, with gentle music playing in the background. Lighting candles helps clear away any negative energy and water is cleansing. You may prefer a shower, in which case make sure it is a long shower, taking time for the water to permeate through your skin and hair.

Go outside into nature by taking a walk, or just standing in the garden. This will help ground you more than you realize and is a form of meditation. Play any gentle music that you feel drawn to that is gentle on your soul.

Honor Your Pet: Support an Animal Welfare Organization

You can decide to make a donation to an animal rescue organization, Humane Society, People for the Ethical Treatment of Animals (PETA), or any animal sanctuary that you feel drawn to. There your beloved pet's name is immortalized and the donation will help other animals. Many organizations have unique ways to honor and remember our pets.

For example, they may create an engraved stone that you can receive a picture of, or a memorial that appears on their website.

Seek Spiritual Support

You can talk to Archangel Azrael, who is the Archangel who helps us as we cross over and looks after the people who are left behind grieving. Archangels are there to help us; all we have to do is ask for their help. They are not restricted by time and space and inhabit the higher realms of existence.

Find Healing through VortexHealing

VortexHealing meditations and healing will help shift your pain without the use of medication.

VortexHealing is about change and the transformation of consciousness at a deep causal level. It works on the mental, physical, emotional, spiritual, and karmic bodies. More information about VortexHealing as related to pets and grieving is available on my website, www.healingpeopleandpets.com.

***

On the spiritual side, our beloved pets are out of pain and suffering, and can run and play just as they did when they were young, hale and hearty. It's on the human realm, which is the densest energy of all, that we have difficulty with loss and letting go. Your beloved pet who is released is free. It's we who have the residue of all the pain and sorrow, and try to come to terms with the loss.

However, even when we know consciously that our beloved pets are at peace, the realization that we won't be able to physically touch, hold, or cuddle them again is extremely difficult to bear. It's the loss of the physical form. Just know that the spirit transcends, but they are still with us in our hearts and our whole being.

Our beloved pets will come and visit or you may dream of them. They know you are in pain and want to ease your grief.

Philippa Kingsley

Each companion animal who enters our life is there for a reason; they are here to help us learn from them. There is no coincidence as to why we choose the companion animals, our beloved pets. Or is it that they choose us? All we have to do is open up our hearts and listen. Animal energetic vibration is on a different channel to our own. Stay quiet long enough and you tune into it. The animals are our teachers; they love unconditionally, the true essence of pure Divine Love.

We all come from Source and we go back to Source to live in Oneness. It takes the animals to open our hearts and give us the ability to show grief for the pure unconditional love that they give us. Just know that your beloved pet is always with you until you meet again, when you yourself cross over the Rainbow Bridge.

8. UNCONDITIONAL LOVE

VOGUIE

It's taken us 30 years to groom you.
You are now ready.
We didn't let you have children because you have much work to do.
We let you have dogs to understand unconditional love.
You will be shown.
Keep trusting.
You will be shown.

Channeled July 27, 2007

Here lies my beloved Voguie, whose spirit soars…

These were the words that were channeled through me in the early hours of the morning that was to be my beloved Voguie's last in his present form on earth. I got up, showered, washed my hair, and put on a long white dress, a sign of purity. I had not consciously acknowledged this was the day, but unconsciously I knew.

On Wednesday, September 22, 2004, my beloved Voguie transitioned from his physical body. He had kidney failure since the beginning of June. I had to give him shots of fluid every other day and he was on a special diet. I also worked with a homeopathic veterinarian in Connecticut and wonderful vet here in Atlanta, who adored Voguie. On the previous Friday he had just stopped eating, and became very tired. I just knew in my soul this was the beginning of the end.

I took him to the vet on Monday and the levels were as high as they were at the beginning of June. I was in utter torment and had been using the services of an animal communicator in Pennsylvania for some time. An animal communicator is able, through telepathy, intuition and technique, to understand and translate thoughts, pictures, and feelings from our animals. I knew that Voguie would tell me what he wanted me to do and when. On Wednesday, I just knew in my soul that this was the day, as I had been channeled in the early hours of the morning.

At two-thirty in the afternoon I spoke to the animal communicator and she told me that Voguie just wanted to leave his body. He had been trying to leave through the portal but couldn't quite do it himself and needed my help. He also wanted the sound of classical music as he transitioned from his physical body.

Through my tears and sorrow I knew it was an act of total love and unselfishness that I had to orchestrate. Voguie found a spot in the garden; I knew that he was not going to move from there. I had opened all the sliding doors to the garden with the sound of classical music billowing out into the air. The vet and her assistant came at five o'clock.

We were all in the bushes with him, crying: I, my husband, Martin, our other dog, Cosmo, the vet, and her assistant. At five thirty-eight he left this world.

I knew that I had to have him with me at this time. Placing him in his basket with his white blanket, we put him in the kitchen by the fire place, surrounded by Burmese wooden monk statues. I lit candles and incense; it looked like he was lying in state.

Our neighbors, Jack and Linda and their standard poodle, Dukie, came by to pay their respects and say goodbye. Voguie, Cosmo, and Dukie had been like The Three Musketeers—totally integrated into our family, and a triangle of love and fun.

Martin and Cosmo finally went to bed, exhausted and emotionally drained. I mounted a night vigil for Voguie. Talking, meditating, and crying. It was something I was guided to do on a soul level. This was the first time that I had experienced the loss of someone who I totally loved unconditionally.

On Thursday, September 23, at eleven o'clock in the morning, we buried Voguie, wrapped in purple silk in his basket, in our garden by the pond. Our garden looked so beautiful, peaceful and serene. My Thai friend Tip came by and we said some Buddhist chants.

I was in a totally depressed and debilitated state for three months, and so was my darling Cosmo; we both mourned the physical loss of our Voguie. At that time, Martin didn't understand me at all, and it certainly caused friction. Everyone deals with grief in different ways at different times and stages in life.

My heart was breaking, but I knew that I had no choice but to release Voguie. He's in the light, and when it is time we will meet again. In the meantime, I know that he is forever in my heart, guiding me as he once did in previous lifetimes.

Ode to Voguie on a Charmed and Cherished life

You were such a dignified English gentleman, an English cocker spaniel with total breeding and manners. I fell in love with you the moment I set eyes on you when you were a puppy. You touched the hearts of everyone you met, just by being you.

My beloved Voguie, you told me yesterday that if I assist you I am doing an act of love and unselfishness. This was one of the hardest things for me to do, but I knew that it was what you wanted. Compassion and letting go was the lesson you taught me; I knew in the end it was best for you and it was what you wanted me to do for you. You are the child we never had. The pure undiluted love I have in my heart for you will never dull. You were part of us and our lives, in Holland and Atlanta. All the memories, all the good times, all the fun and the cuddles. Forever in our hearts and souls.

You are forever eternal, just in a different dimension. I will see you, feel you, smell you again; when it's time for me to leave this world, I know you will come and get me, and we'll be together forever across the Rainbow Bridge.

Voguie, I know you love me utterly, and you trusted me to do the right thing. I was in total torment and emotional inner turmoil. I wanted the decision to be yours, because I didn't think I was capable of assisting you. You have been my guide in the past, you guided me yesterday, and you will guide me in the future. I made a quantum leap of faith, an act of love and unselfishness, to release you from this earthly coil. I didn't know how I could do it, but we are guided by forces higher than our human perception. You said yesterday that what I have done for you is an act of love and unselfishness. And so it is.

I celebrate your life and our life with you. You enriched our lives; it's no coincidence that you came to share your time with us, as it was meant to be. Thank you again my darling, dearest, cherished Voguie.

9. UNCONDITIONAL LOVE

COSMO

My darling Cosmo transitioned from her physical body on Friday, October 23, 2009, at home, assisted by our caring veterinarian, with the scenario unfolding of myself, Martin and the vet crying buckets of tears.

What can I say about my beautiful darling Cosmo? A golden angel with four legs. A gentle disposition, but definitely a mind of her own. If she didn't want to do something, she wouldn't, and nothing could persuade her to change her mind.

She left me at a time when I was extremely challenged emotionally, as I had just lost my beloved father in May, and it became clear to me that she would be leaving me the same year. I just didn't know which month or how the scenario would unfold, as we had been living on borrowed time, and every day was a gift to be appreciated.

Thankfully, Martin, my husband, was much more aware and involved than he had been previously. He had seen the whole grief process unfold when I returned to Atlanta from London after my father's transition.

After Voguie transitioned in 2004, Cosmo had changed from being a fun-loving dog, part of a team, with Voguie as the alpha dog, and became a shadow of her former self. A great depth of sadness was so apparent in her eyes. As if the weight of the world was on her shoulders, she physically aged overnight. She mourned the loss of Voguie with every part of her being.

Cosmo and I now created a strong bond of pure love and giving to each other, and she grew into her own identity, with a stronger sense of herself. With Voguie gone, there was no longer a buffer to hide behind; she had no choice but to come out of her self-imposed shell, and she transformed into the alpha dog. Cosmo now wanted the attention all for herself, which she felt she had earned and deserved. She was asked if she would like a new dog to enter our family but she didn't. She adored Dukie, her friend from down the street, and that was all that she wanted.

Health problems arose. Her liver enzymes changed for no apparent reason. She had always been so healthy, but things started to break down. Many physical problems manifested. She would also lie on Voguie's grave in the garden for periods of time. She didn't want to go on, but it wasn't her time to leave.

I was in touch again with the animal communicator who shared the intricacies of Cosmo's thoughts. I still used the same veterinarian as before, and enlisted the help of a holistic vet here in Atlanta. I was beside myself, doing everything possible that I could.

In 2008 mammary gland cancer appeared. She let us know that she didn't want anything invasive done to her, and I respected her wishes. Again, the pre-grieving period set in. Knowing, but not wanting to believe, yet the awareness of the outcome was always under the surface.

My heart was heavy; I received this lesson and these words from Cosmo: "Let me take you energetically through this journey."

By the beginning of October, 2009, it was obvious that she couldn't keep everything going. She was out of her body for most of the time and I knew that I would again have to utilize my strength to help release her soul from her body. During the next two weeks all our friends that knew Cosmo came to say goodbye to her. She wanted to leave her body from home, where she would be surrounded by love and familiarity.

I called the vet and arranged that Friday, October 23, would be the day. Friday dawned, and she went into the garden and tottered around, as if saying goodbye to all the shrubs, trees and her favorite places. She came back and lay down in the living room on her cushions by the window, surrounded by all her furry toys, and closed her eyes. Martin and I were holding and cuddling her and each other, joined in this act of surrender and release.

Our vet came at noon, sad to the core, as this was the end of an era for us all. At twelve-thirty p.m., our darling Cosmo's soul flew to the higher realms of being.

We wrapped her in pink Thai silk. The color pink denotes love, and as Cosmo was a girl and she loved pink, this was fitting. We moved the big cushion to the kitchen with Cosmo, and it was her turn to lie in state.

I sat with her the rest of the day and into the night, as I had with Voguie. Candles, incense, and meditations, so empty into the void. The words were channeled to me to be spoken at her burial. Friends came the next day to share the moment, to honor her, and pay their respects. We buried our darling Cosmo next to her beloved Voguie.

I sit here sharing Cosmo's story as she channels it to me and how she wants her story told, with the realization that this will be Grace for all those who need awareness and help to get through loss and letting go of those that we love.

***

This was channeled through me and read at Cosmo's burial on Saturday,
October 24, 2009

Our darling Cosmo,
You touched my heart, you touched my soul with who you were,
truly a special gift from the Divine.
You were more than just a pet,
you were our furry four legged child
with a strong mind of your own and a bundle of love.
You were so courageous during this last year when diagnosed with cancer.
You didn't want surgery and I respected your wishes.
When everything started to break down
you decided you no longer wanted to suffer.

Transitioning from the physical form is a process itself.
You showed me energetically how the process unfolds.
Nothing is black and white, so many shades of grey.
Everything is as it's meant to be.
If we listen to our pets
we observe how much more knowledge they have,
so much more than us human beings.

The lesson is Surrender and Release.
To put theory into practice is a lesson well learned.
Acceptance of all that is.

Dukie, the standard poodle was part of our family.
The days when it was *The Three Musketeers*,
Voguie, Cosmo and Dukie are no more,
The times when all three were racing around the pond
will never be forgotten
Cosmo and Dukie had a grand love affair which has endured,
with Dukie bringing Cosmo a single pink rose,
a token of their love.

We shared a journey, beloved Cosmo.
We grieve for what we had, what is no more in physical form.
But you are eternal, always deep in our hearts.

I know that Cosmo is now reunited with Voguie.
He came to take her to the angels
in the angelic realm where she now rests.

Love is the most important thing in the world.
Dogs give unconditional love.

Our darling Cosmo, you rest here next to your beloved Voguie.
THEIR SPIRITS SOAR

MY FATHER AND MY PETS

10. HELP IS AT HAND

Channeled from my father, Voguie, and Cosmo August 2010

Are there coincidences in life? There are no coincidences, but there is such a thing as Divine timing. When we are at a juncture in our soul's journey when we are ready, we are guided in spirit by those that we love, by our guides, and the angelic realm. We are guided to do certain things, and thoughts come through us. We meet certain people, books fall off shelves, we think about someone and they call us, or we call them; the list is long when one starts to think about all the things that seemingly "just happen."

August 1 was my father's birthday. In May I had returned from London after *the stone setting*, or *unveiling*, as it's called in U.S. —the Jewish ritual that takes place one year after a death to dedicate the gravestone. I was feeling intense sadness when suddenly the thought popped into my head to give myself an Angelic card reading using Doreen Virtue's Archangel Card Deck. The first card I chose was from Archangel Azrael, the Archangel who helps people when they first transition from their bodies, and also comforts people who are mourning the loss. The card read *Hello from Heaven*. I knew it was a special message for me from my father, and I then felt comforted and fine that day.

Ten days later, still feeling down and deflated, I went to the Phoenix and Dragon metaphysical bookstore in Atlanta, where I give monthly VortexHealing talks and group healings. I had no real reason to go except it just felt right. I was drawn to the animal communication book section. When I looked at all the titles, the ones that resonated with me were written by Penelope Smith, who has been teaching and using her skills for over thirty years. She had also taught the animal communicator I worked with. I bought three books, and then signed up for the upcoming animal communication course that Penelope would be teaching in September.

My own birthday is September 12, and I realized that Voguie and Cosmo's birthday present to me was for an energetic spurt of extra awareness to formalize and learn the process of animal communication in order to help companion animals and their owners.

After reading Penelope's book, *Animals in Spirit*, something shifted and resonated within me. Interestingly, a friend had previously asked me to look after her dog during her vacation. I had said no because I didn't feel ready to bring another dog in my home. However, the universe decided I was ready; a short while later, a client and friend of my husband, Martin, was going on vacation, and asked if we could look after their dog, Chelsea.

Chelsea is a labradoodle who looks more poodle than doodle! She has a fabulous smile, white poodle-textured fur, and sports a poodle cut. Quite glamorous! I had met her a few times and resonated with her.

I felt a momentary panic and trepidation, but something pushed me to agree to Chelsea being with us, although I had become used to looking after myself, with my own routine. I didn't want anything disrupting my life again.

Chelsea arrived early Friday morning, a gorgeous, loving friendly dog with pure open energy. I melted. I took her into the bedroom with me, where she jumped up on the bed, and we cuddled up, spoon style. I realized there was a deep, aching, empty hole inside me that had been left by the transition of my father, Voguie, and Cosmo, and then our neighbor's dog, Dukie, who had transitioned in December, 2009.

During the next few days, Chelsea reminded me of Voguie, with her intense eyes that seemed to look deep into my soul, and dramatic licking—pure Voguie. The cuddles and warmth of female energy were pure Cosmo. Of course, you can imagine where she slept, in between Martin and me!

The night before she was due to go home, I felt sad. She had opened up my heart again. The whole time that she was with us I was in *mummy mode* full throttle, cooking for her, cuddling her. She was pure love personified! Again, it was all about loss for me, and I cried intensely after she left the next morning.

That night, in bed, I cried, and then the realization came of how she had touched me and made me know that I could feel again. My time with her had awakened pure unconditional love in me, which had been lying dormant. Feelings may lie dormant while we heal, but they never go away; they arise like a phoenix out of the ashes when the time is right. I understand the path that I am on and know that with Divine timing, the right dog will appear for me, as did Chelsea, who was a spiritual catalyst for change.

I received a visitation from Voguie, Cosmo, and Dukie:

We are helping you from the other side. Just feel us; we are around you. Voguie, Cosmo, and Dukie send their beloved Philippa, Martin. and Linda love, light, and licks for always.

Love is eternal and so are we.

45

11. GIFTS FROM VOGUIE AND COSMO

Doggy Update - September 2011
Voguie and Cosmo keep sending me gifts of dogs to look after.

Many people ask me, "Why don't you get another dog?" They say that it doesn't seem right for me to be "dogless." Anybody who knows me knows the love that I have for dogs and cats, and is somewhat perplexed.

A pattern has appeared in our lives, and there is no coincidence. Starting with Chelsea, the labradoodle (more poodle than doodle!) who awakened my dormant unconditional feelings of love, followed by a friend's dog, Hero, the pattern picked up steam with Rumo and Bibi, the wheaten terriers. Then came Gally and Ollie, the standard poodles, an adorable white furry bundle of love called Bucky, plus two angelic Pomeranians, and a couple of furry felines. I do not go out looking for this, but dogs and cats keep appearing for me to pet-sit, from either friends or clients.

It is a "win win" situation for me and all the beautiful dogs that come to stay with us. They each get to have a five star experience, with home-cooked organic food, based on their dietary needs, and an abundance of love and cuddles, as I tend to put my life on hold and cater to their every whim. Their owners have the satisfaction of knowing that their furry children are being looked after in a loving, caring environment.

These dogs and cats have touched my heart and my soul, with their unconditional love and the very essence of who they are, each with their own personalities and characters.

What is so interesting is that the arrival time of each of these dogs does not overlap at all. I know that whenever I need extra loving, Voguie and Cosmo decide that it is time for my unconditional dose of love!

The true story that I will now share with you proves that no matter how big or small, no matter what the form, pure love takes precedence over all.

We have an exquisite pond that Martin built, filled with koi and bullfrogs. Every evening in the summer we could hear the sound of the frogs calling to each other. Every dog that stayed with us was fascinated by the sounds emanating from the pond. An awareness of life in every shape and size was all around in our magical garden, which was lovingly and creatively designed and cared for by Martin.

This past August, Martin woke me up early in the morning to come and look at something in the garden and would not tell me the reason. What he showed me, on the lawn by the side of the pond, was the lower torso of a large bullfrog. Next to it was a small frog, which was clearly its baby. The baby frog did not move and was obviously in shock. We knew that the frog had not been killed by a heron, which sometimes frequents ponds in our area, as ours is kept covered with wire mesh as a deterrent. We have had hawks all around, and one of them must have swooped down and grabbed the large frog as it sat on top of the mesh covering the pond. We could think of no other explanation.

As the morning progressed, I kept on going out to check on the baby frog, worried that it, too, would die, as it had been out of water for many hours. It had changed position and was swatting flies that came to it. I communicated with the frog and knew it was grieving the loss of its mother, which was obvious to see. I did some VortexHealing and angelic healing on the frog to release it for the highest good.

In the early afternoon I went out to the garden again. The frog had turned around again, and was facing the lower torso, with its left hand on the torso. I felt the frog's pain and loss of its mother, and the grieving that was happening. I was picking up the communication and energy of the frog; I couldn't stop crying for the loss of the baby frog's mother. Again, I did some more intense healing for this baby frog, asking that the frog be kept safe and be relieved of its suffering.

Another hour went by. I had a friend from England staying with me, and it was time for me to take her to the airport. With a heavy heart, I went out to the pond, and the baby frog was not there. I felt relieved, and knew intuitively that all the healing that I had done on its behalf had been heard.

Later, Martin came home and buried the remains in the woods. He has seen the baby frog a few times since, so that I know that it is still in the pond. I know that I was honored and aware enough to have been shown the most unusual situation of a baby frog mourning the loss of its mother. Loss is loss, grief is grief, and even though we know that the laws of nature are there for a reason, how often do we get to see such an unusual scenario unfold and be shared with a human being?

There is no coincidence in the unfolding of this scene. The baby frog wanted his story told. How do I know? After writing these words, I went to the pond and there he was. He didn't move. I crouched down and we sat at looked at each other for what seemed an eternity. He thanked me for sharing his story so that others would understand the bond and love that all animals have for each other, irrespective of the physical form. Again, it's we, the human beings, who need to realize that love transcends all. Awareness of All That Is and pure love defines all beings.

The image of this baby frog with its hand on its mother will forever be etched in my memory.

I know that the healing path that I am on is guided by Source, with the help of Voguie and Cosmo. Everything is unfolding now as it is meant to be. When I am guided to have a dog again, it will all happen in Divine timing.

Love, caring, and sharing will open your soul to all the magic that the universe has to offer. Sharing the combination of animal communication, VortexHealing, and unconditional love with all the animals that appear in my life is my chosen path, now and forever.

OTHER VOICES

12. WHERE IS MY MOTHER'S VOICE?

Channeled in January and May, 2009.
Final channeling in my friend Teresa's kitchen.
Her dogs and cats are keeping me company!

September 2011

Where is my mother's voice? I am her voice.

Grief manifests in many forms. My dearest mother, Betty, is trapped in her physical body in a timeless state of limbo. Alzheimer's disease is her challenge and ours.

Further and further into the abyss of no return
she gently navigates around her home,
not knowing which way to turn, what questions to ask,
the darkness, yet awareness on some level that all is not right.
The crushing crescendo of fear always felt,
names being a total mystery of who and how they relate.

Luckily, at this time, my mother still lives in the home that she and my father shared. My brother, Richard, and sister-in-law, Marion, live five minutes from my mother. I have an amazing sister-in-law; she is a compassionate person, has great depth and understanding of the situation, and was willing to take on the practical considerations of all that this entailed. We have had professional caregivers living with my parents, and then my mother, for the past seven years, beginning when it became obvious to all that my mother just couldn't take care of anything or anyone anymore.

Alzheimer's is a living death. To watch someone that you love who was a fully-fledged member of the human race transform into a vegetative state is extremely difficult to watch, let alone live with, on a day-to-day basis.

She lives totally in the past, babbling gibberish at times, talking to her parents, sisters, and my father, all no longer in physical form. She has mood swings and drifts in and out of sleep, yet physically, for her age, which is 88 years old, she is quite fit. It's just the mind that has opted out of life.

Being in her own surroundings and having full-time attention from professional long term caregivers, along with my brother and sister-in-law's frequent visits, certainly help her quality of life. This may, of course, change, as the concentrated pressure on the caregivers is immense, living day in and day out in this challenging dimension.

Each situation is different, and many family caregivers eventually have to admit a realistic defeat, and have to put a beloved parent in an assisted living facility or nursing home. Relief and guilt often go hand in hand as caregivers realize that their own health and mental states have to be taken into consideration, in conjunction with what is best for their parent.

I last saw my mother when I went to London in April. Even though she could not have a coherent conversation, the moment she saw me, the vacant look in her eyes cleared and she lit up with a knowing. Although trapped in the prison of her mind, like in a vacant parking lot, on an energetic level, she knew who I was; it was just the mind that could not converse. I will never forget that look of awareness. I sent her pure unconditional love and VortexHealing. It's all I could do, but knowing that pure love transcends all helps to make the situation bearable.

It's taken me to now to realize that I am her voice. The sadness is that my mother never found her voice. As a child she was always scared and petrified of life; this carried on to her adult life. She was the youngest child in a financially comfortable, large, and loving family, with her mother (my grandmother) as the matriarch.

One chapter of her story, which has had a profound effect on me, shows how fear, combined with lack of self- worth, can totally paralyze people. My mother loved the arts; she was a pianist, she painted, spoke French, was an avid reader of all literature, and was absolutely brilliant at writing. However, in London, prior to World War II, it wasn't considered important for a girl to go to university (college) to further her education or have a career.

A large, prestigious international publishing company ran a national competition, and the prize was a much-coveted job at the company. It would be a once-in-a-lifetime chance for the winner.

My mother won the competition. All that was needed was the mere formality of the publisher meeting the winner. The meeting was arranged. However, my grandmother had other ideas, and told my mother that she couldn't go. She made up a story that my mother was needed to go and babysit her niece. This was ludicrous, as there was an entourage of staff in the house. My mother canceled the appointment and wasted the opportunity of a lifetime, all because of fear and lack of self-worth.

Over the years, on numerous occasions, both my father and I asked her why she didn't just tell her mother that she was going to the appointment. She never replied.

When fate comes knocking at the door, we are given choices; either we accept the gift with open arms and Divine Timing, or through fear and lack of self-worth, we don't take the opportunity as it is offered.

People come into your life for a reason, a season, or a lifetime, in whatever capacity. We all have our own karmic path to tread, and many people have such pain and sorrow etched into their belief system that it can cause emotional or physical manifestation. It takes great strength of character and courage to release this negativity. Learning how to forgive yourself, or an issue, will enable you to move forward, and make a quantum leap of faith in your life on the miraculous journey of the human soul. Keep faith, trust, and belief in yourself. Ask for help; you will be facilitated and empowered during your journey along the spiritual path to discover your life purpose. The realization that all you have to do is to commit to yourself is a simple act of awareness and love.

I will always remember, on one occasion back in 2005, my mother saying to me, "What a lovely girl you are." Although I am hardly "a girl" anymore, these words of love and approval from my mother's lips will never be forgotten. VortexHealing showed me how to forgive, and I have truly forgiven my mother and myself for many things that unfolded over the years; my only regret for her is that I am sorry she never found peace, happiness, or harmony in her own life. I hope that in her next life she commits to herself.

I am guided to share her story with you; I know that she would like to have spoken about it too, as she was eloquent of speech and open to new ideas. She just didn't have the inner strength to put it into practice.

Each week I speak with her by phone for about two minutes. Even though she cannot converse, I tell her, "You are my mummy, I love you very much, and I always will." I energetically connect to her and send her love and light forever.

Now you know why I am her voice.

13. A CHILD'S GRIEF

Grief affects children. Adults who are caught up in their own grief, or who deny themselves the basic compassion of feeling grief, often forget to check in on their children.

Children suffer the loss, too, whether it is of a parent, grandparent, family member, friend, or pet. They just don't always know how to express it verbally with an adult. Children and teenagers often act out their grief.

Grief is usually not talked about openly in Western society. Children sometimes don't want to upset their already upset parents, or the upset parent doesn't want to upset their child, with the result of nobody discussing or opening up to their feelings of loss. In fact, a full sharing of love and communication is needed for both parties, not stiff upper lip syndrome.

I had just returned to Atlanta from London and was mourning the loss of my darling father. I received a phone call from a client to whom I been recommended to help her five-year-old granddaughter who had recently lost her father. I spoke to the child's mother, who told me that her daughter, Hannah, was one of twins, but the other twin was able to cope.

Hannah was in a terrible state of grieving. The whole family had just moved back to Atlanta, and each member was in various stages of grief due to loss of a husband, father, and son-in-law. Hannah's mother was extremely worried about Hannah; she had been to see various counselors and therapists, and nothing had worked. In desperation, they had called me, as they felt that perhaps a different approach was needed.

I realized that even though I was totally immersed in my own grief and was officially not working, I knew that there was no coincidence that this situation with Hannah had arisen at this specific time. There is a lesson in everything in life. I also knew that dealing with a child would be totally different than dealing with an adult. For one thing, there is the attention time span. One cannot have a long conversation with a child. I knew that I would have to play games with her, and just casually throw out a question, couched in appropriate terminology, when the time felt right.

I met Hannah at her home, and we bonded immediately. We just played games in her bedroom, and I spoke to her on a general level to ascertain her mindset. Hannah was a very sensitive and spiritual child who is what I would call a Crystal child. As Doreen Virtue describes in her book *The Crystal Children*, a Crystal child is one who was born from 1995 onwards. This child has the raised energetic vibration for the collective need of the earth at this time.

After I saw Hannah a few times, building a friendship and relationship with her, and gradually finding out how she felt, things moved to the next level. On my next visit her mother was very upset, saying that Hannah was acting out her pain by crying, shouting, and turning inward, and was in a terrible state. I went to her bedroom, and spoke to her gently; finally she unburdened herself and started to cry. I held her, spoke to her, and then did VortexHealing on her. I asked

Archangel Azrael to help her. Archangel Azrael is the archangel who helps people at the moment of transition from the physical body, as well as the people left behind who are grieving. Hannah fell into a deep sleep and had a release from all the pain that her little five-year-old body was carrying.

After that day she improved at a fast rate. It was like a new little girl appeared. I still kept seeing her, and saw the progress that she was making. Everybody in the family was ecstatic. Today she is eight years old. We remain connected, and a close friendship has ensued with everyone in the family.

About one year later, I helped one of the older children deal with his grief. I was able to talk to him and showed him that writing things down would also help release the pain. Again I used VortexHealing and invited him to Archangel Azrael to help release his pain. Today, he is well adjusted and now has found that it feels good to laugh in life.

When you see or feel a child in pain, reach out to help them in any way that you can. Let your heart open to how they may be feeling. Imagine how you would feel if you were that child, not knowing how to express your pain and sorrow of loss. Find a way to help them open up and share their feelings. They need to hear that you are a safe haven of comfort and nurturing in which to express their grief.

When I was called on to help Hannah, I knew that on a higher level something was playing out. To be able to help someone else, even when you are in pain, is giving a gift of love.

Love, Caring, and Sharing

14. DRAMA OF LIFE

For all who choose to listen

Channeled and written to my cousin's son Saul
September 2011

The spiritual bond that we have happened gradually. Given the family dynamics, combined with friendship and the spiritual quest that you are on, it becomes powerful and can grow from an acorn to an oak in timeless fashion.

Our bond started with your pet snake! You used to keep it in your bedroom in a large heated glass container. I was in London, and came to dinner at your home; we talked, realized that we had things in common, and that we understood each other. I explained to you about VortexHealing and animal communication. We went upstairs to your bedroom to meet your pet snake.

We sat on the floor facing the snake. What was extremely interesting was that the snake unfurled itself and gracefully slithered over to my side of the glass. It then opened its mouth extremely wide several times and seemed totally focused on me. You were as surprised as I was. I remember joking that it either liked me or thought I was dinner! The snake seemed totally transfixed with me and I started to communicate with it. The three of us were connected at that moment in time, you, your snake, and me.

After I returned to Atlanta, when you wrote to me with your realization that your beloved cat Calypso was getting older in years, and the prospect of losing her loomed on the horizon in your thoughts, you had questions about the meaning of life, death, spirituality and the cycle of life. I answered you with openness and fullness of soul: you can prepare yourself mentally for grief, however, when a loss or transition occurs, all the floodgates open up and an avalanche of emotions rise up and pour out from the depth of your whole being. Even though you know that it is part of the cycle of life, you feel the momentous intensity of loss. Loss is loss and cannot be underestimated.

When your beloved cat transitioned from her physical body, you were distraught and e-mailed me. I lovingly explained to you about the process of death and grief, and how it's always hard for those of us who are left behind, but your cat Calypso was now released. I was touched when you wrote to me, "I feel so honored to have someone like you in my family." We all need someone in our lives who understands the various sides of our character and personality and who won't judge us as we grow and change throughout the years. It has transpired that I am your spiritual mentor, with the added dimensions of friend and family. I am also guided to share with you that there is a reason why you are extremely sensitive and spiritually orientated: you are an early Crystal child (Virtue 2003). This means that you have a raised energetic vibration and were born at this time for the collective karma of the earth as it goes through great transmutation.

Life is like the pieces of a jigsaw puzzle, all scattered until they come together to form one large picture. My other analogy is that we are all spiritual pawns on a chessboard and that the Divine moves us around and positions us to enable us to think for ourselves. We are given choices as to the moves that we make on the chessboard of life.

You are moving forward with your life, always have faith, trust and belief in yourself and in life itself. When situations arise in life, which, of course, they will, realize that they are just part of what you are here to learn. Just know that the human realm is the densest energy of all the different dimensions of time and space. When a *drama* unfolds, what we as humans usually do is believe that it is real. It certainly feels real, and we are often challenged with this drama. We tend to add energy to the drama, and it compounds more and more energy, until we have built it or the situation out of all proportion. This seems easy to say and to see, but it can be extremely difficult to remove oneself from a dramatic scenario while it is in the process of unfolding.

It has taken me some time to truly ripen and resonate with Divine timing as it unfolds. As spiritually aware as I am, I know that I am still a human being, with all the trials and tribulations that being human brings to my life. Challenges don't just miraculously melt away into the background. They have to be seen for what they are, learning lessons of life.

I look at a life drama, certainly feel the emotion, but then I step back and realize that I am in a play. It's as if I am on the side of a stage, like an understudy watching the actor in the center of the stage and the drama unfolding. The difference is that I am outside myself, watching myself act out the drama on the center stage. It's not really real, it's just that we give credence to the *drama* and our role. We do this lifetime after lifetime, compounding more and more energy to the *drama*.

At a soul level we are real. We have our imprinted, genetic, and ancestral karma, and then we have our own soul learning karma. Who we were in millions of other lifetimes is who we always were and who we always will be at our soul level. Whether you were in male or female form, whatever country, or wherever you decided to incarnate, it was to learn what you needed to learn.

At this time in the universe we are given individual and group choices; what we choose to do with our lives will help us in the world, as everything is now illusion. We need to ask, *what is real and what is not*? When we look at an actor on stage or in a movie we believe for the time in the illusion that they are portraying; however, illusion is all that it is. I share with you that the most important thing in your life is to be true to yourself. Go with your instincts and they will never let you down.

I am guided to write this to you now because I know that at a core level you understand. I am sure that you don't understand all this at a surface level, but at a future date and time in your life, as you shift your consciousness and grow your spirit to your full purpose, these teachings will resonate with you and you will look at these words and understand All That Is.

MUCH LOVE AND LIGHT FOREVER

MY FAVORITE ANIMAL ORGANIZATIONS

My personal experience at Kindred Spirits Animal Sanctuary in Santa Fe, New Mexico, was profoundly moving. Kindred Spirits is an eldercare and hospice for dogs, horses, and poultry. They help and care for animals that people deem no longer important in their lives.

My husband Martin and I have also been volunteering at Atlanta Pet Rescue, which provides us a different dimension and perspective of the wonderful work that this organization does for dogs and cats, giving them a second chance for a loving home.

Perhaps you have seen *Dogtown* on television. This National Geographic Channel series tells the story of Best Friends Animal Society, in Kanab, Utah, the largest animal shelter in the United States, and a leading proponent of the "no-kill" animal shelter and rescue movement. Best Friends became known nationally for rehabilitating and training the pit bulls rescued from Michael Vick.

I also highly commend and respect the rescue and sanctuary organization called Farm Sanctuary in Watkins Glen, New York, which has a sister rescue and sanctuary in California. There are guest visiting programs where you can meet and bond with a rescued animal.

The work that People for the Ethical Treatment of Animals (PETA), well known in the United States and internationally, raises awareness about the lives of all sentient beings we call animals, with the realization that all animals, in any physical form, have feelings; they can love unconditionally, feel pain and fear, and deserve our love and respect.

For more information on the work of these organizations, please visit their websites:

- www.kindredspiritsnm.org
- www.atlantapetrescue.org
- www.bestfriends.org
- www.farmsanctuary.org
- www.peta.org

RESOURCES

www.healingpeopleandpets.com

www.vortexhealing.org

Karen Adler, Editor: karenadler@gmail.com

www.SRwalkerdesigns.com (front cover design)

Photography: www.erinbrauerphoto.com

Penelope Smith, animal communication specialist, www.animaltalk.net

www.angeltherapy.com

Virtue, Doreen. The Crystal Children. Carlsbad, CA: Hay House, 2003.

FREEDOM TO BE FREE IS FREEING